Easy Piano

ENCANTO: Music from the Motion Picture

Disney

ENCANTO

Original Songs by Lin-Manuel Miranda

ISBN 978-1-70515-960-6

HAL•LEONARD®

Visit Hal Leonard Online at
www.halleonard.com

Contact us:
Hal Leonard
7777 West Bluemound Road
Milwaukee, WI 53213
Email: info@halleonard.com

In Europe, contact:
Hal Leonard Europe Limited
42 Wigmore Street
Marylebone, London, W1U 2RN
Email: info@halleonardeurope.com

In Australia, contact:
Hal Leonard Australia Pty. Ltd.
4 Lentara Court
Cheltenham, Victoria, 3192 Australia
Email: info@halleonard.com.au

CONTENTS

THE FAMILY MADRIGAL

Music and Lyrics by
LIN-MANUEL MIRANDA

With a Latin groove

Vocals 2nd time only Drawers! Floors!

Doors! Let's go!

MIRABEL:
This is our home, _ we've got ev'ry gen-er-a - tion. So full of mu - sic, a
My ti-a Pe - pa, her mood af-fects the weath - er. When she's un-hap - py,

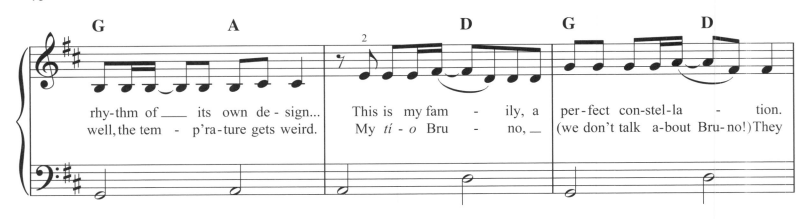

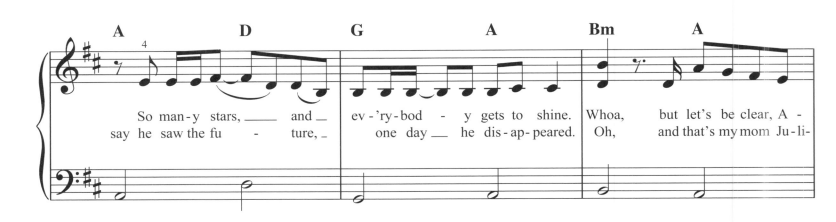

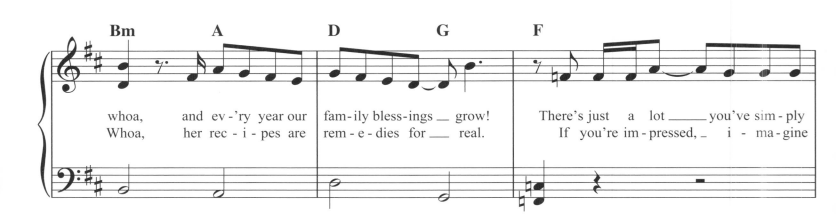

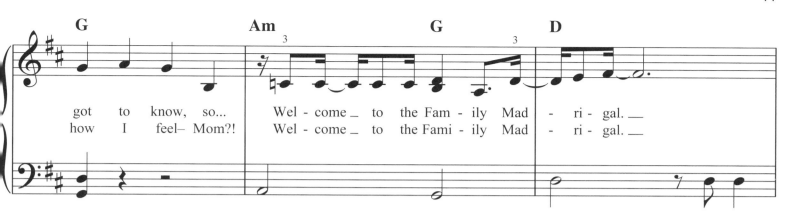

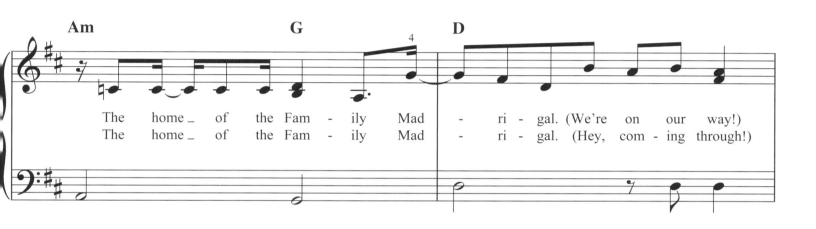

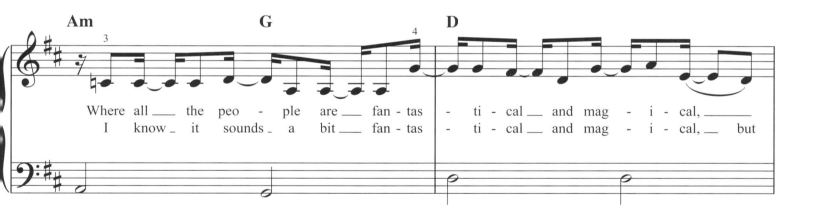

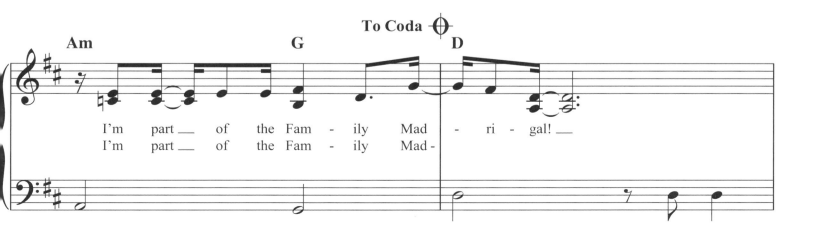

TOWN KIDS:

Oh my gosh, it's them! What are the gifts?! I can't remember all the gifts. But I don't know who is who.

MIRABEL:

Alright, alright, relax.

TOWN KIDS:

It is physically impossible to relax!

D.S. al Coda

Tell us everything! What are your powers?

TOWN KID:

JUST TELL US WHAT EVERYONE CAN DO!

MIRABEL:

And that's why coffee's for grownups.

CODA

- ri - gal! __ Two guys fell in love with Fam - ily Mad-ri - gal! And

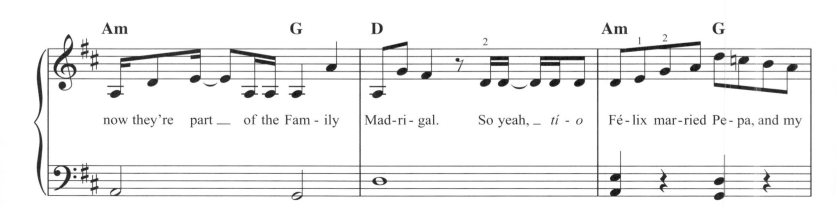

now they're part __ of the Fam - ily Mad-ri - gal. So yeah, __ *tí - o* Fé - lix mar-ried Pe - pa, and my

dad mar - ried Ju - li - e - ta, that's how A - bue - la be-came an *A - bue - la*

Mad - ri - gal! Let's go, let's go!

ABUELA ALMA:

We swear to al - ways help those a - round ___ us,

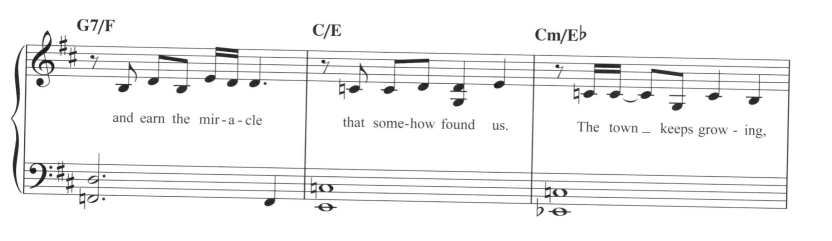

and earn the mir - a - cle that some-how found us. The town ___ keeps grow - ing,

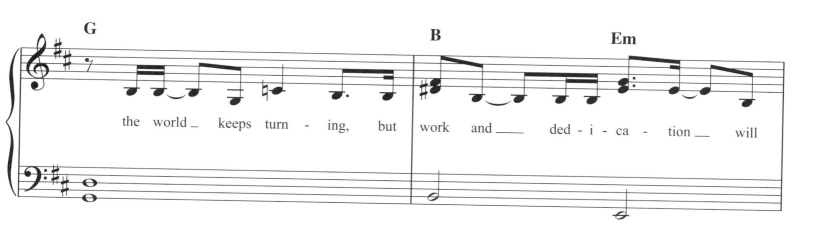

the world ___ keeps turn - ing, but work and ___ ded - i - ca - tion ___ will

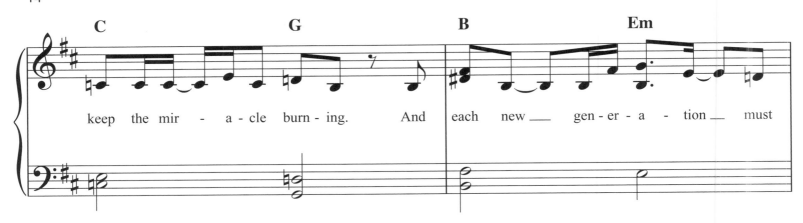

keep the mir - a - cle burn - ing. And each new gen - er - a - tion must

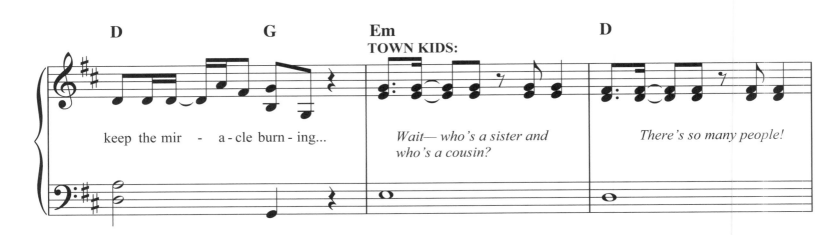

keep the mir - a - cle burn - ing...

TOWN KIDS:
Wait— who's a sister and who's a cousin?

There's so many people!

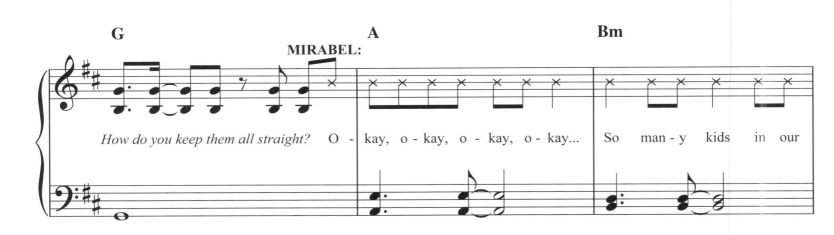

How do you keep them all straight?

MIRABEL:
O - kay, o - kay, o - kay, o - kay... So man - y kids in our

house so let's turn the sound up! You know why? I think it's time __ for a grand - kid round up!

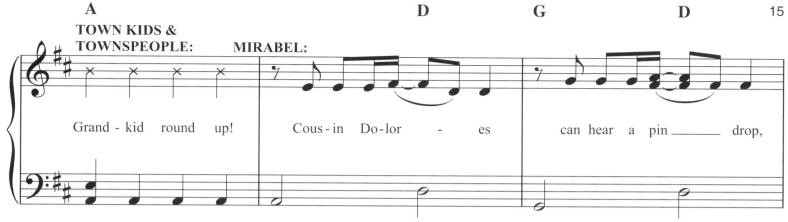

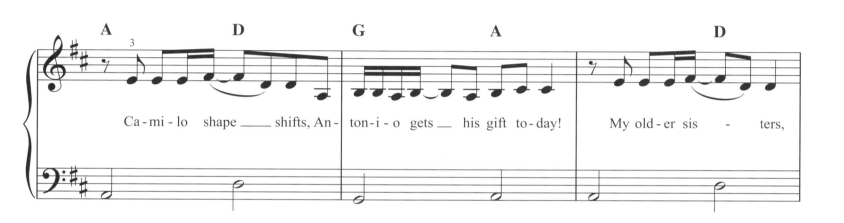

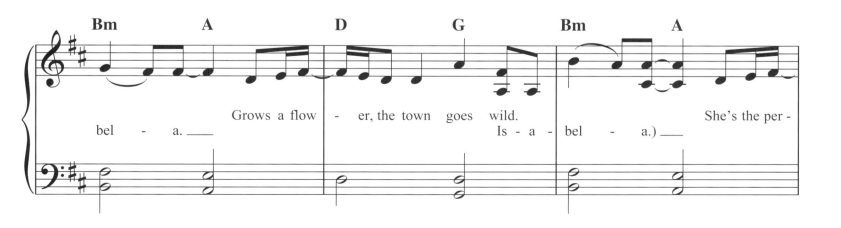

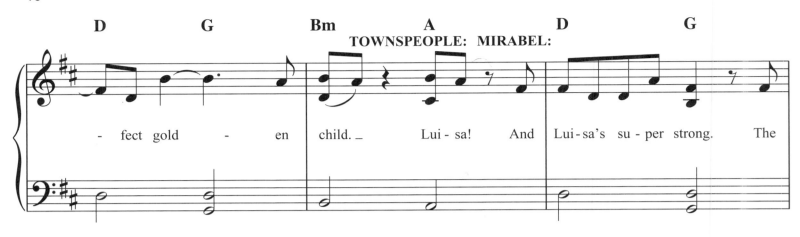

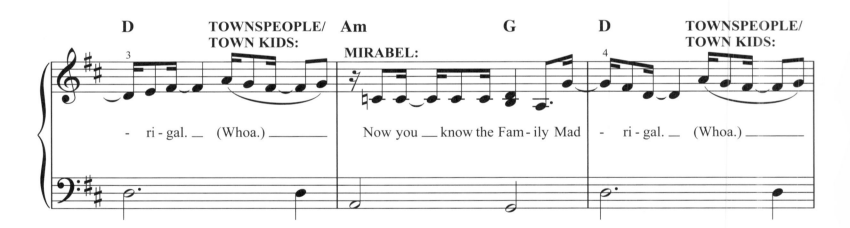

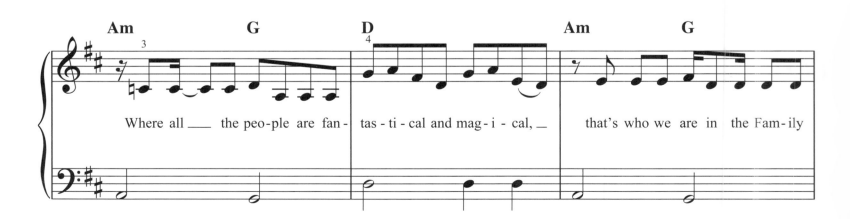

so just ___ to re - view, the Fam - i - ly Mad - ri - gal, (But what a - bout

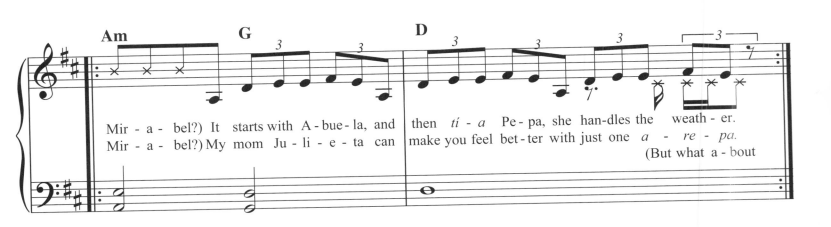

Mir - a - bel?) It starts with A - bue - la, and then *tí - a* Pe - pa, she han - dles the weath - er.
Mir - a - bel?) My mom Ju - li - e - ta can make you feel bet - ter with just one *a - re - pa.*
(But what a - bout

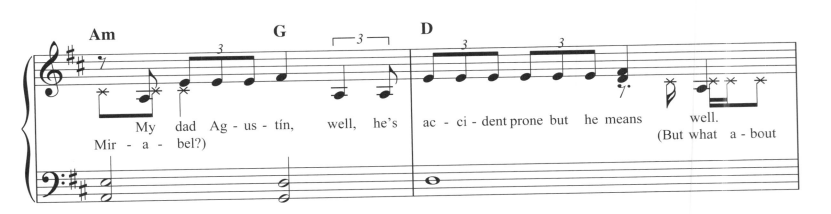

My dad Ag - us - tín, well, he's ac - ci - dent prone but he means well.
Mir - a - bel?) (But what a - bout

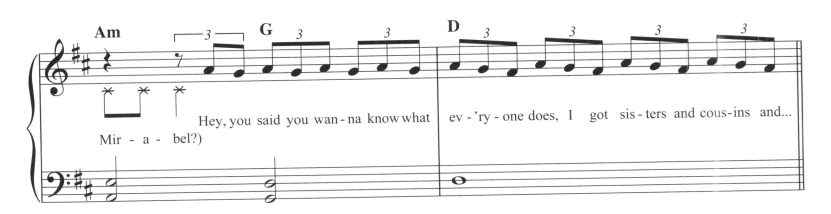

Hey, you said you wan - na know what ev - 'ry - one does, I got sis - ters and cous - ins and...
Mir - a - bel?)

(Mir - a - bel!) My *prim-o* Ca - mi - lo won't stop un - til he makes you smile to - day!
(Mir - a - bel!) My cous - in Do - lo - res can hear this whole cho - rus a mile a - way!

Look! It's Mis - ter Mar - i - a - no, hey! You can mar - ry my sis - ter if you wan - na. Be -
(Mir - a - bel!)

tween you and me, she's kind of a pri - ma don - na. Yo, I've said too much and thank _ you but I real - ly got - ta
(Mir - a - bel!)

ABUELA ALMA:

go! My fam - ily's a - maz - ing! And I'm in my fam - ily, so... well... MIR-A-BEL!
(Mir-a bel!) (Mir-a-bel!)

WAITING ON A MIRACLE

Music and Lyrics by
LIN-MANUEL MIRANDA

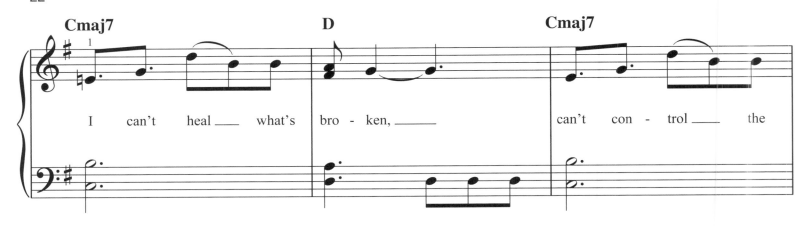

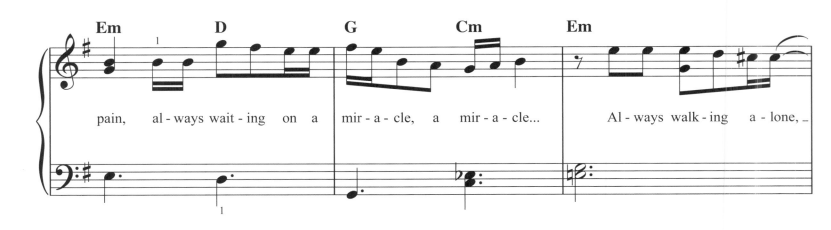

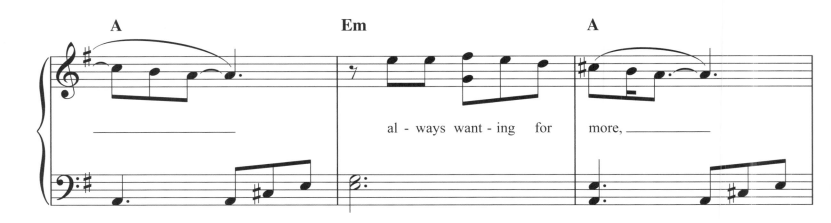

like I'm still at that door ___ long - ing to shine ___ like

all of you shine. ___ All I need is a change, ___

all I need is a chance, ___ all I know is I

can't ___ stay on the side. ___ O - pen your eyes, o - pen your

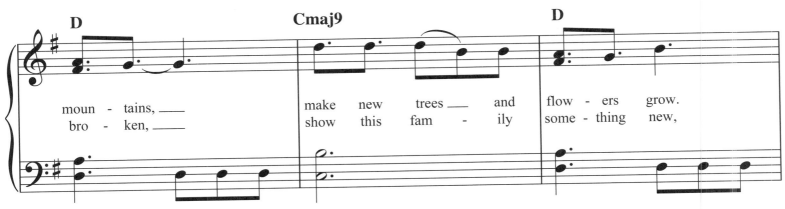

mir - a - cle, so here I go...   I am read - y! _____   C' - mon, I'm read - y! _____

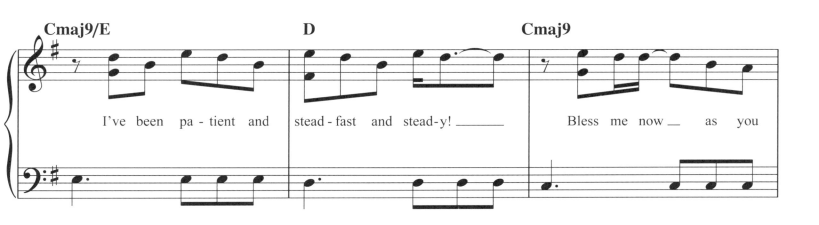

I've been pa - tient and   stead - fast and stead - y! _____   Bless me now __ as you

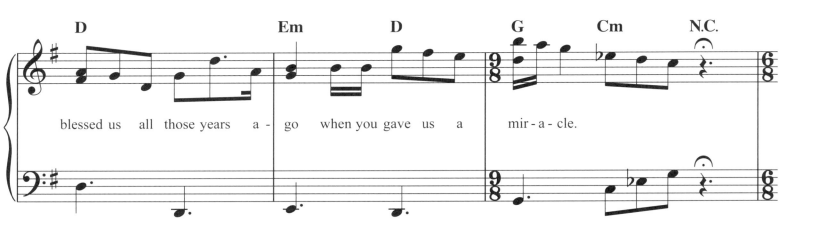

blessed us all those years a - go   when you gave us a   mir - a - cle.

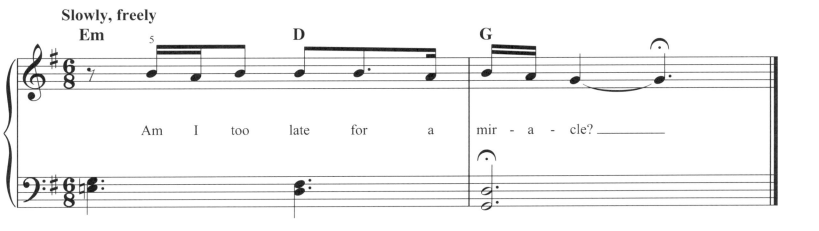

Am I too late for a   mir - a - cle? _____

SURFACE PRESSURE

Music and Lyrics by
LIN-MANUEL MIRANDA

Dia-monds and plat-'num, I find 'em, I flat-ten 'em, I take what I'm hand-ed, I break what's de-mand-ed, but...

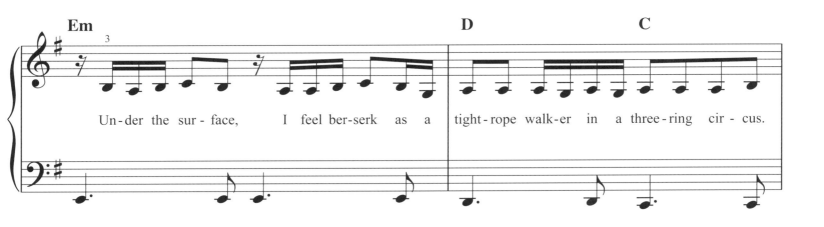

Un-der the sur-face, I feel ber-serk as a tight-rope walk-er in a three-ring cir-cus.

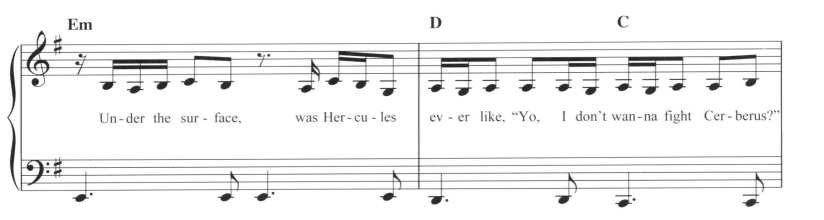

Un-der the sur-face, was Her-cu-les ev-er like, "Yo, I don't wan-na fight Cer-berus?"

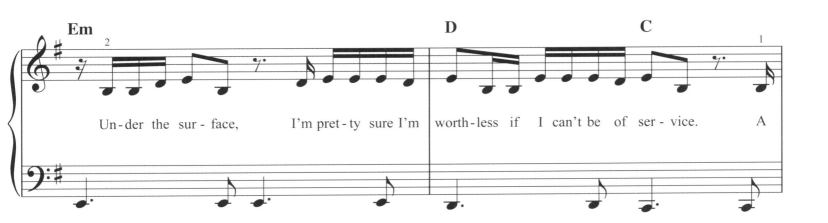

Un-der the sur-face, I'm pret-ty sure I'm worth-less if I can't be of ser-vice. A

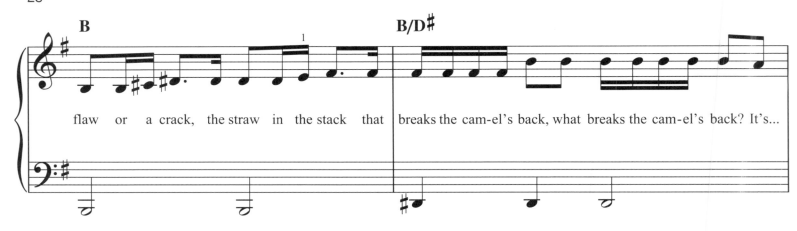

flaw or a crack, the straw in the stack that breaks the cam-el's back, what breaks the cam-el's back? It's...

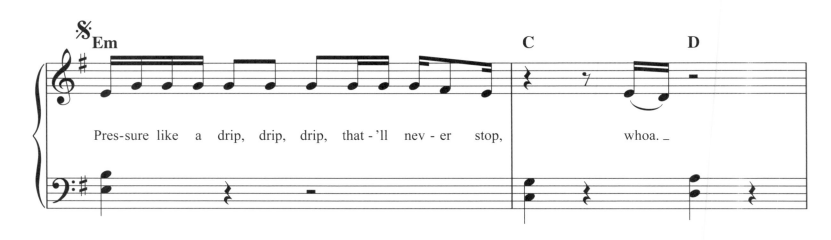

Pres-sure like a drip, drip, drip, that-'ll nev-er stop, whoa. _

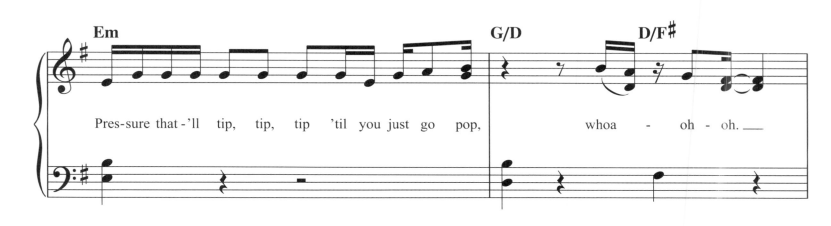

Pres-sure that-'ll tip, tip, tip 'til you just go pop, whoa - oh - oh. ___

Give it to your sis - ter, your sis-ter's old - er, give her all the heav-y things we can't shoul - der.
Give it to your sis - ter, it does-n't hurt, _ and see if she can han-dle ev-'ry fam-'ly bur - den.

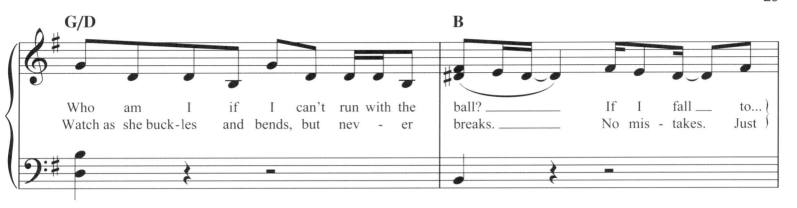

Who am I if I can't run with the ball? _____ If I fall ___ to...
Watch as she buck-les and bends, but nev - er breaks. _____ No mis - takes. Just

Pres-sure like a grip, grip, grip and it won't let go, whoa. _

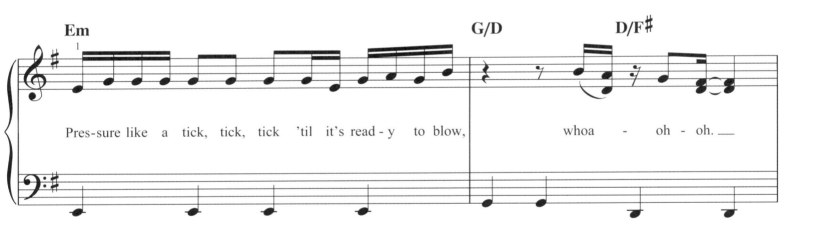

Pres-sure like a tick, tick, tick 'til it's read-y to blow, whoa - oh - oh. __

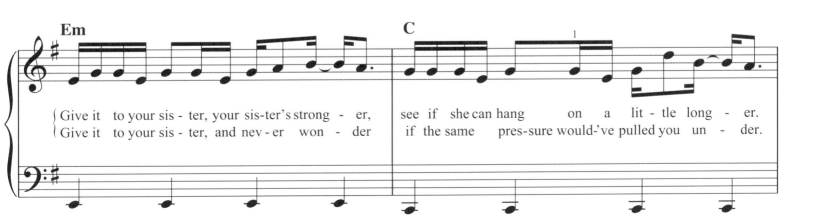

Give it to your sis - ter, your sis-ter's strong - er, see if she can hang on a lit - tle long - er.
Give it to your sis - ter, and nev - er won - der if the same pres-sure would-'ve pulled you un - der.

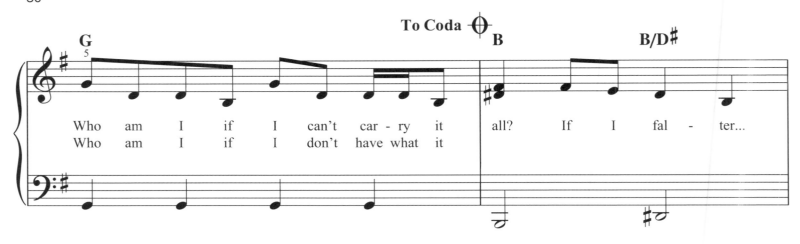

Who am I if I can't car - ry it all? If I fal - ter...
Who am I if I don't have what it

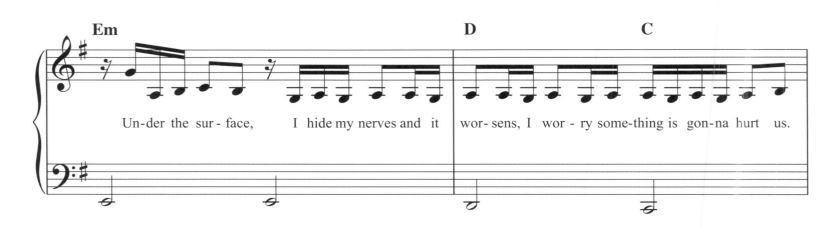

Un - der the sur - face, I hide my nerves and it wor- sens, I wor - ry some-thing is gon-na hurt us.

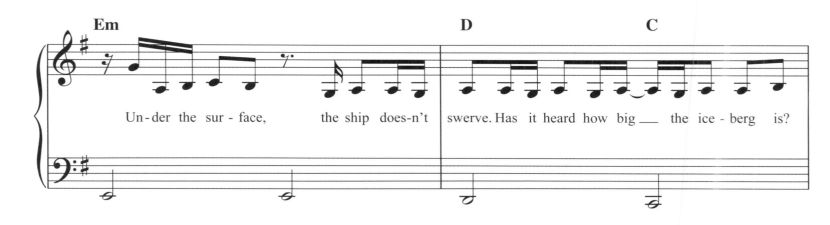

Un - der the sur - face, the ship does-n't swerve. Has it heard how big ___ the ice - berg is?

Un - der the sur - face, I think a - bout my pur - pose. Can I some-how pre-serve this? Line

up the dom - i - noes, a light wind blows, you try to stop it top - pl - ing but on and on it goes. But

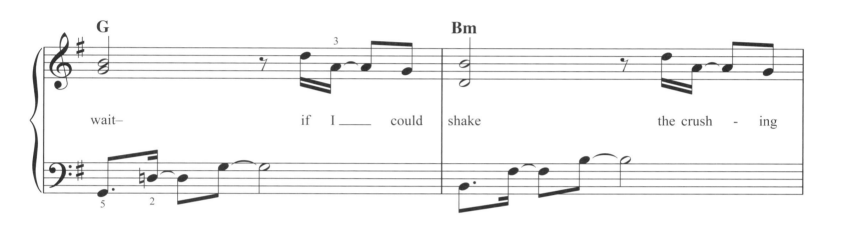

wait— if I _____ could shake the crush - ing

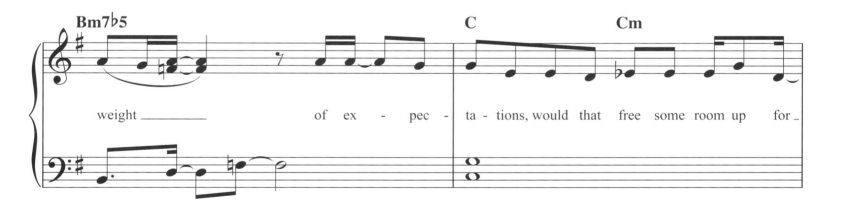

weight _____ of ex - pec - ta - tions, would that free some room up for _

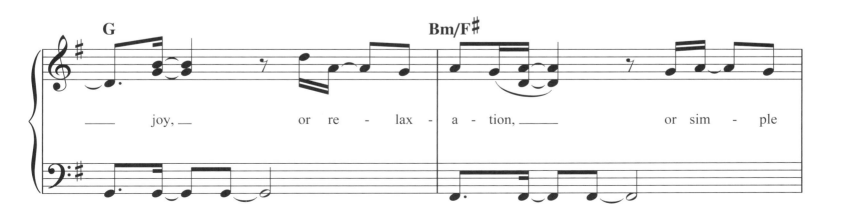

_____ joy, _ or re - lax - a - tion, _____ or sim - ple

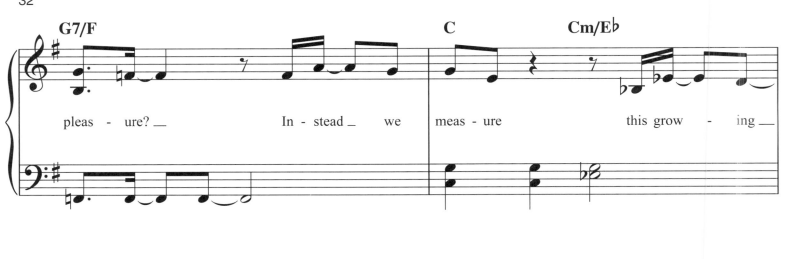

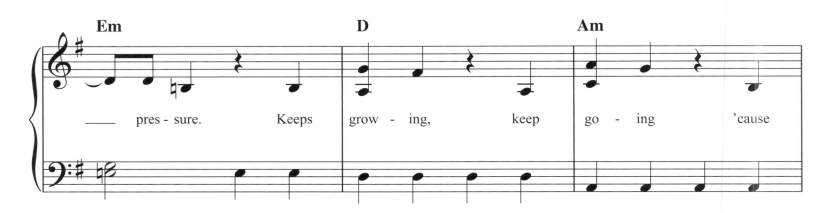

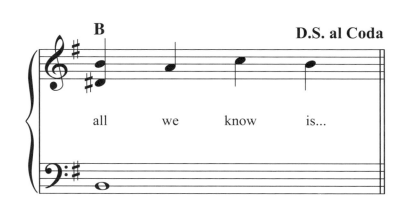

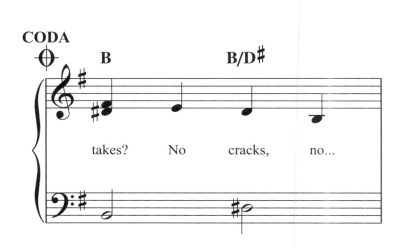

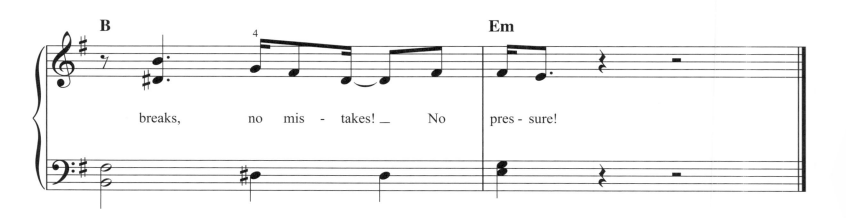

WE DON'T TALK ABOUT BRUNO

Music and Lyrics by
LIN-MANUEL MIRANDA

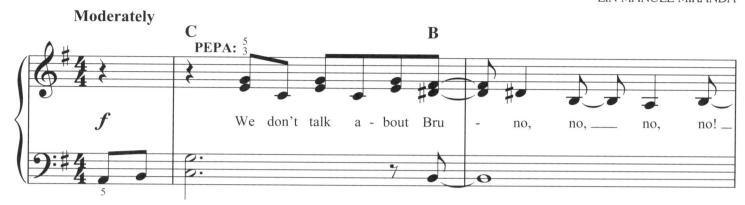

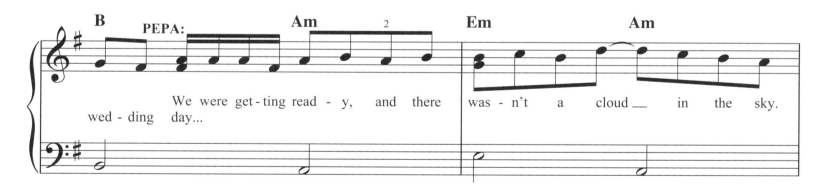

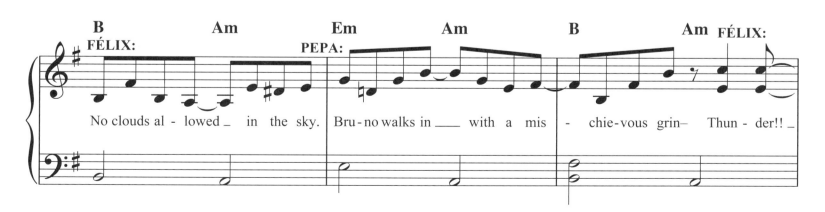

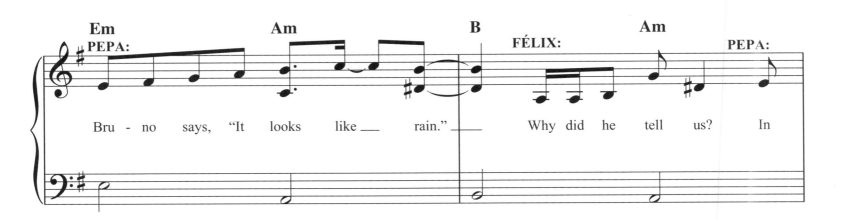

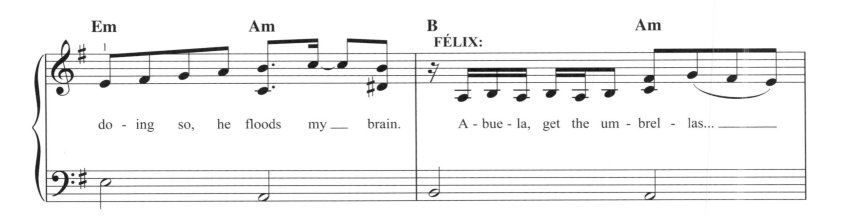

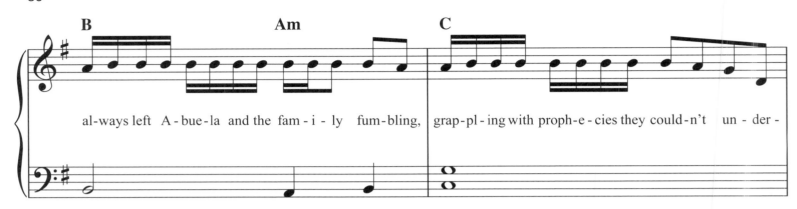

al-ways left A-bue-la and the fam-i-ly fum-bling, grap-pl-ing with proph-e-cies they could-n't un-der-

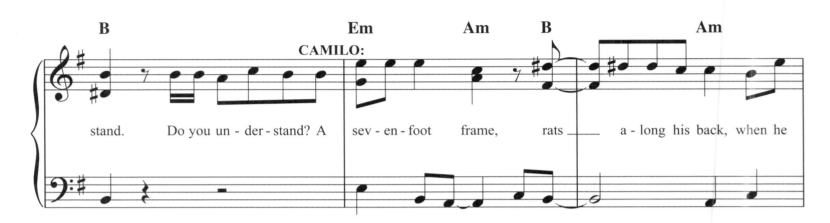

stand. Do you un-der-stand? A sev-en-foot frame, rats a-long his back, when he

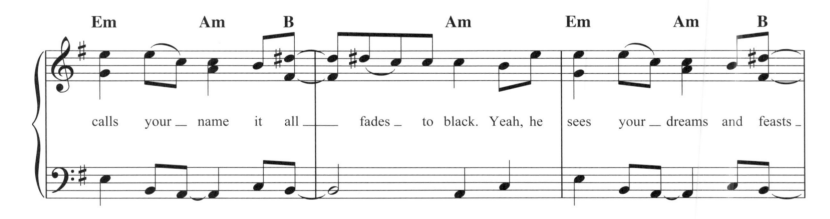

calls your name it all fades to black. Yeah, he sees your dreams and feasts

on your screams. We don't talk a-bout Bru - no, no, no, no!

37

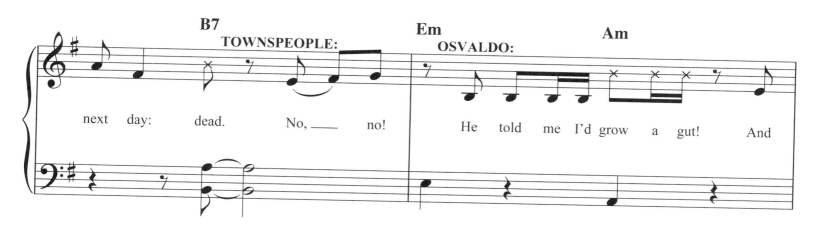

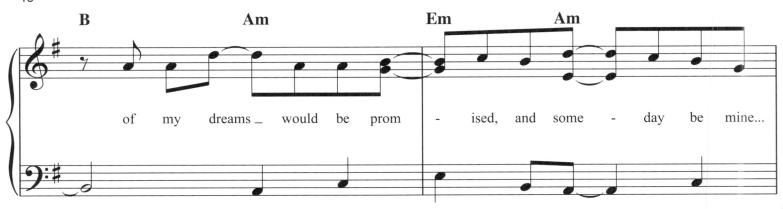

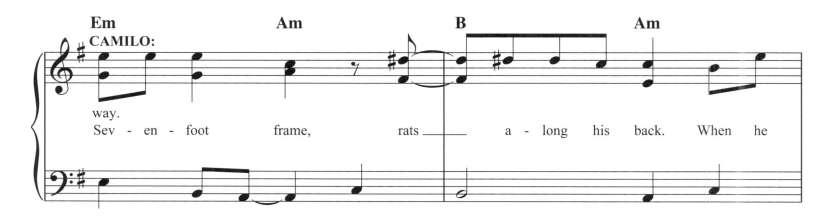

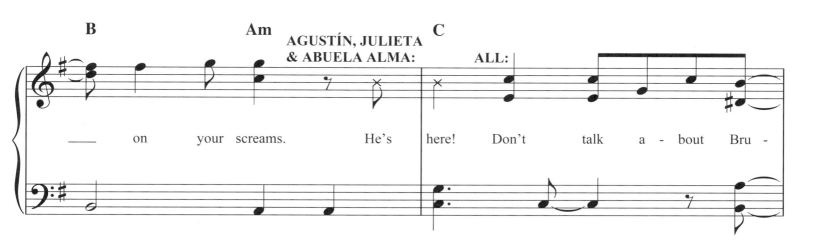

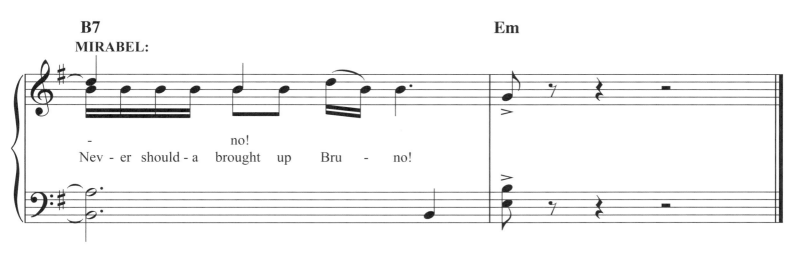

WHAT ELSE CAN I DO?

Music and Lyrics by
LIN-MANUEL MIRANDA

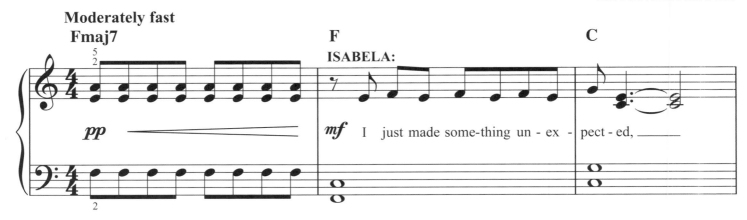

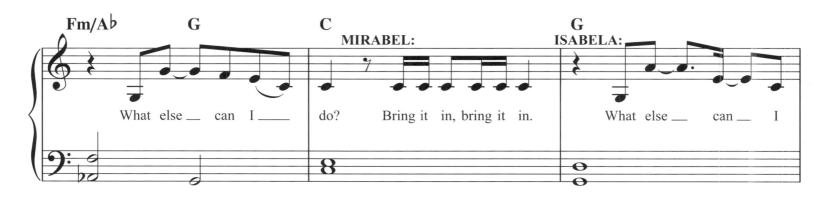

MIRABEL: Am / G / ISABELA: C

do? Bring it in, bring it in. Free hugs! Bring it in, bring it in. I grow rows ___ and rows ___

G / Am / G

___ of ros - es, *Flor de may - o,* by the mile. _____

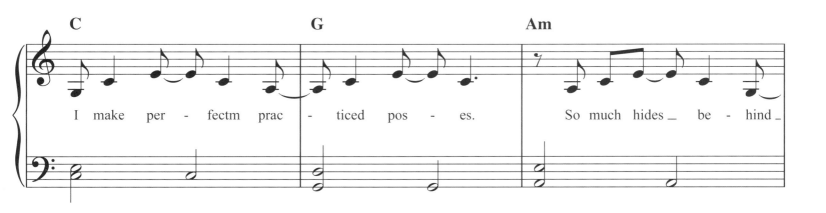

C / G / Am

I make per - fectm prac - ticed pos - es. So much hides ___ be - hind ___

G / A♭ / B♭

___ my smile. _____ What could I do if I just grew what I was feel-ing in the

44

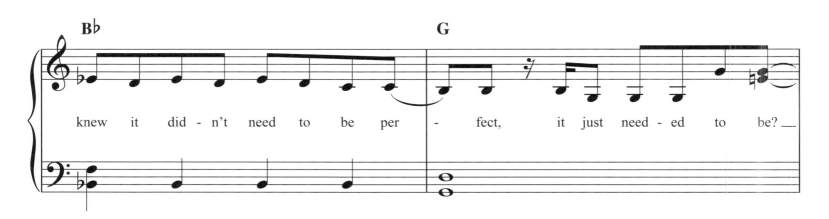

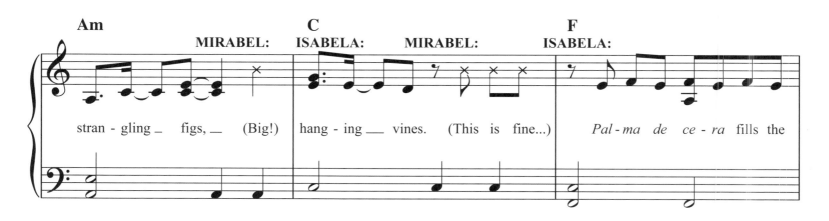

air as I _____ climb _____ and I _____ push through... _____ What else _____ can I _____

do? _____ Can I de - liv - er us a riv - er of sun - dew? _____

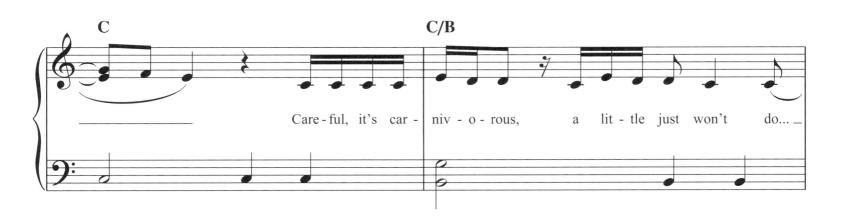

_____ Care - ful, it's car - niv - o - rous, a lit - tle just won't do... _____

_____ I wan-na feel the shiv-er of some - thing new. _____ I'm so sick of

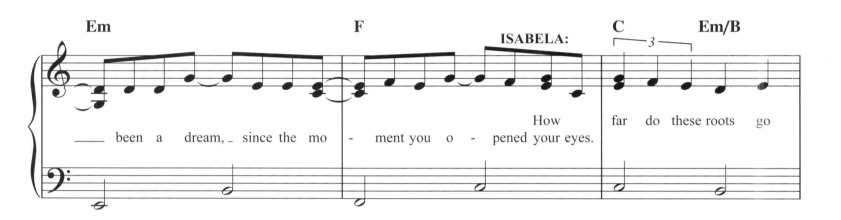

G **F** ISABELA: **C**

___ let's go... ___ A hur - ri - cane of *ja - ca - ran - das,* ___

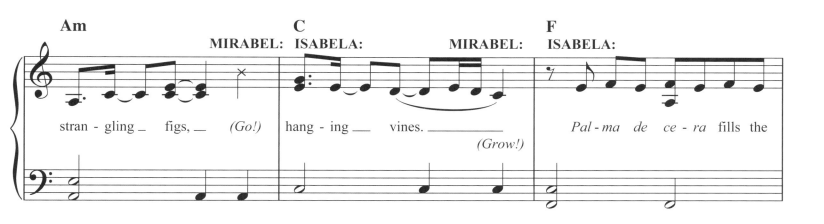

Am **C** **F**

MIRABEL: ISABELA: MIRABEL: ISABELA:

stran - gling ___ figs, ___ *(Go!)* hang - ing ___ vines. ___ *(Grow!)* *Pal - ma de ce - ra* fills the

C **Am** **Fm/A♭** **G**

MIRABEL:

air as I ___ climb ___ and I ___ push through... ___ What else, ___ what else?

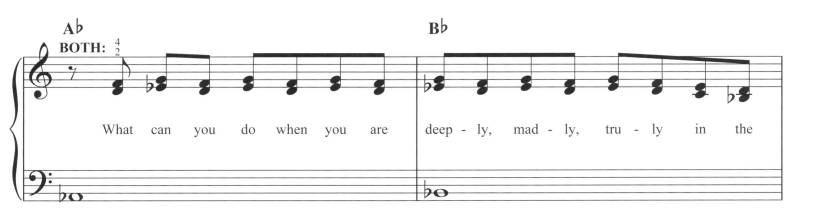

A♭ **B♭**

BOTH:

What can you do when you are deep - ly, mad - ly, tru - ly in the

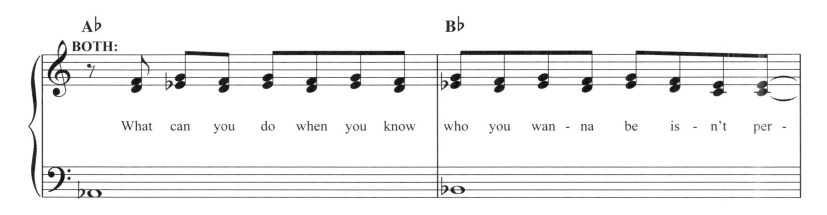

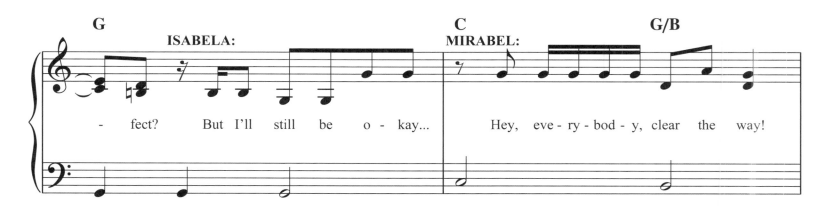

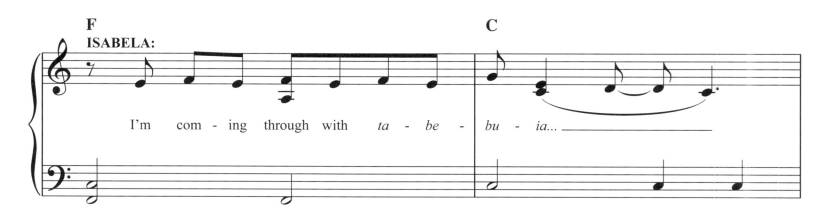

mak - ing ___ waves, _ chang - ing ___ minds. _ The way is clear - er 'cuz you're

here, and well, _ I owe ___ this all ___ to you. _ What else ___ can I ___

MIRABEL:
do? ___
Show 'em what you can do. ___

ISABELA:
What else ___ can I ___ do? ___

MIRABEL:
There's noth - ing you can't do. _

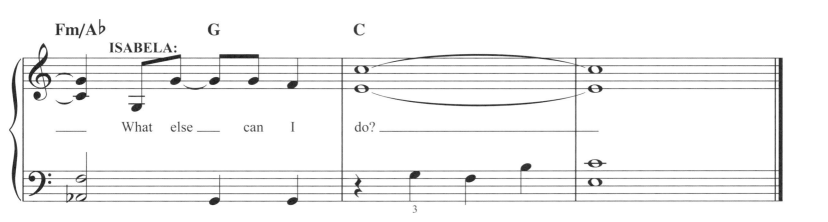

ISABELA:
___ What else ___ can I do? ___

DOS ORUGUITAS

Music and Lyrics by
LIN-MANUEL MIRANDA

Syncopated groove

Dos or - u - gui - tas,
Dos or - u - gui - tas

e - na - mo - ra - das,
pa - ran el vien - to,

pa - san sus no - ches
mien - tras se a - bra - zan

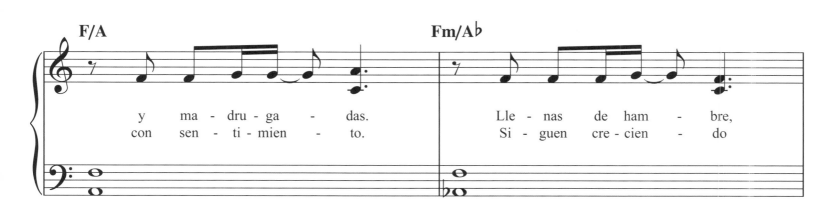

y ma - dru - ga - das.
con sen - ti - mien - to.

Lle - nas de ham - bre,
Si - guen cre - cien - do

si - guen an - dan - do y na - ve - gan - do un mun - do que
no sa - ben cuán - do bu scar al - gun __ rin - cón. El

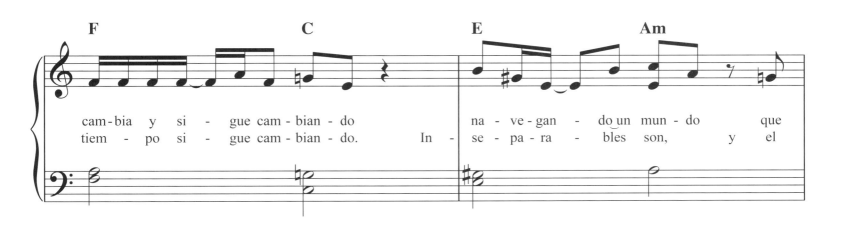

cam - bia y si - gue cam - bian - do na - ve - gan - do un mun - do que
tiem - po si - gue cam - bian - do. In - se - pa - ra - bles son, y el

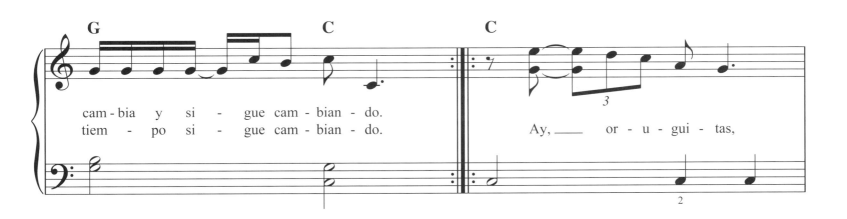

cam - bia y si - gue cam - bian - do. Ay, __ or - u - gui - tas,
tiem - po si - gue cam - bian - do.

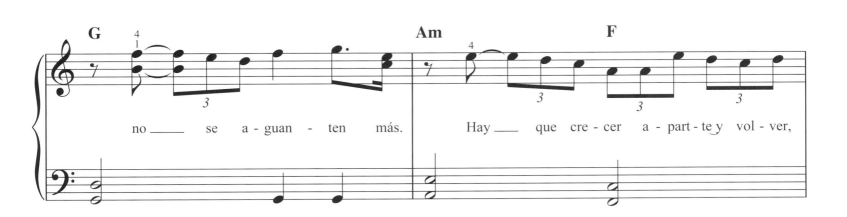

no __ se a - guan - ten más. Hay __ que cre - cer a - part - te y vol - ver,

ha - cia a - de - lan - te se ___ gui - rás. Vie - nen mi - la - gros,

vien - en cri - sá - li - das. Hay ___ que par - tir y ___ cons - tru -

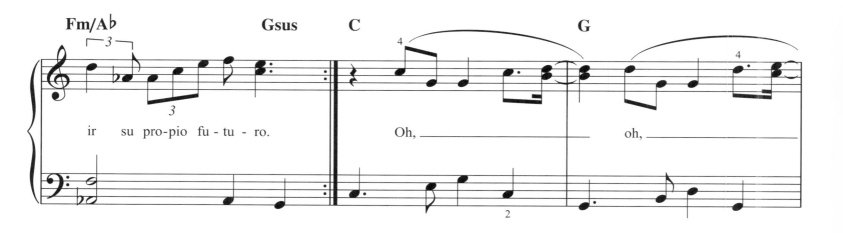

ir su pro - pio fu - tu - ro. Oh, ___ oh, ___

___ oh, ___ oh. ___ Oh,

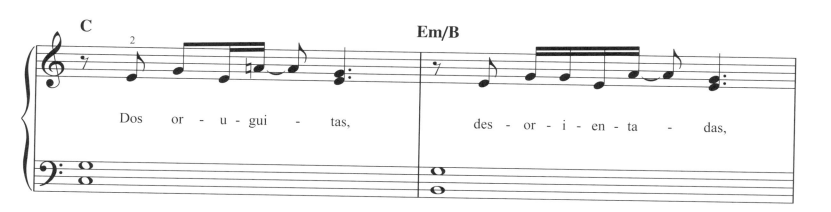

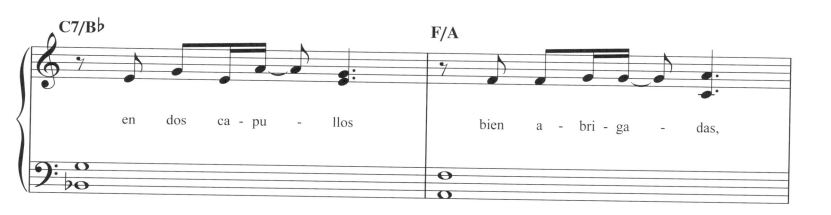

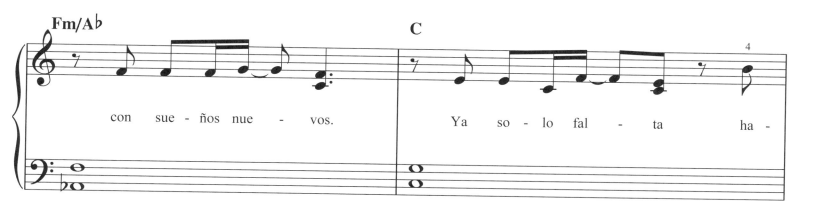

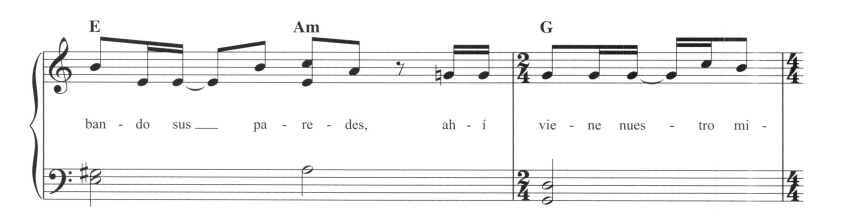

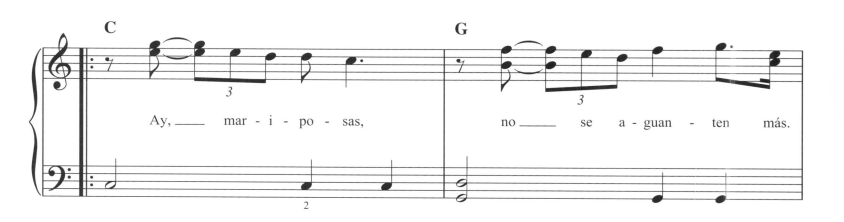

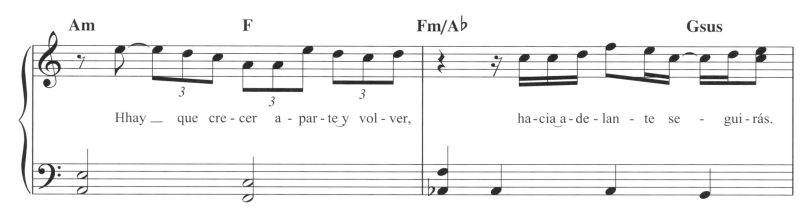

Hhay __ que cre - cer a - par - te y vol - ver, ha - cia a - de - lan - te se - gui - rás.

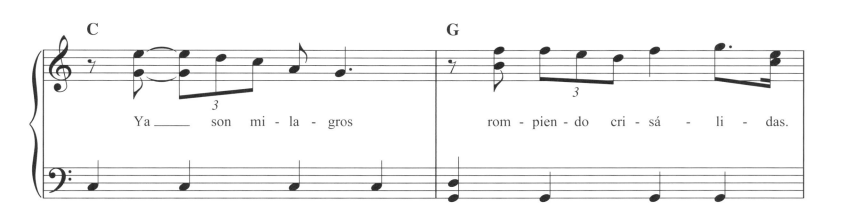

Ya __ son mi - la - gros rom - pien - do cri - sá - li - das.

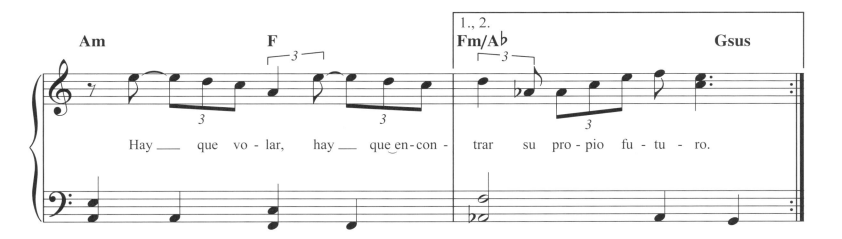

Hay __ que vo - lar, hay __ que en - con - trar su pro - pio fu - tu - ro.

trar su pro - pio fu - tu - ro.

rit.

ALL OF YOU

Music and Lyrics by
LIN-MANUEL MIRANDA

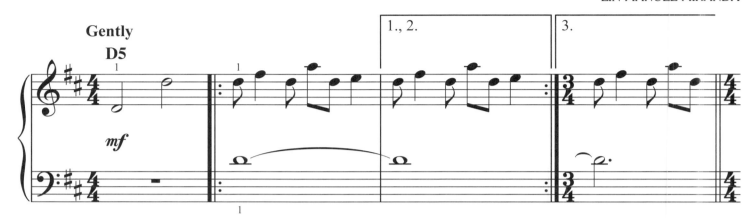

Look at ___ this home, we need a new ___ foun-da - tion. It may ___ seem hope - less,

but we'll ___ get by just fine. Look at ___ this fam - 'ly, a glow-ing con - stel - la - tion

so full of stars, ___ and ev-'ry-bod-y ___ wants ___ to shine. But the

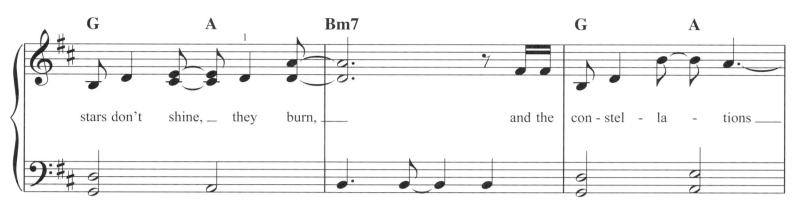

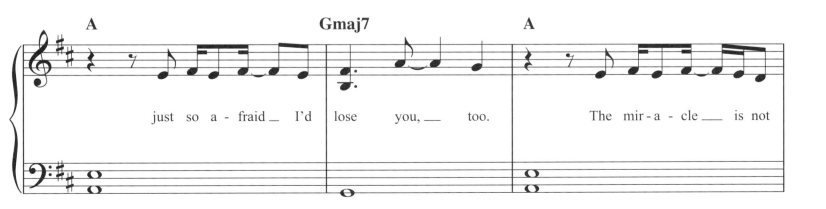

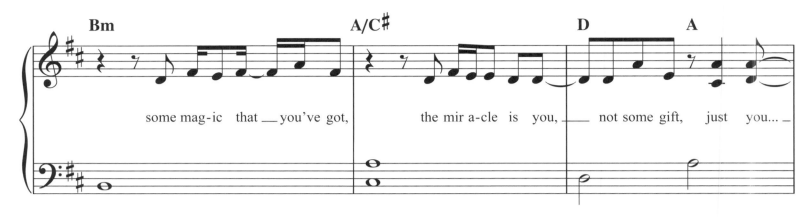

some mag-ic that __ you've got, the mir a-cle is you, __ not some gift, just you...

__ The mir-a-cle is you.__ All of you,__ all of you.__ O - kay so...

we gon-na talk a-bout Bru - no? That's Bru - no! Yeah, there's a lot to say a-bout Bru -

- no. I'll start, o-kay. Pe-pa, I'm sor-ry 'bout your wed-ding, did-n't mean to be up-set-ting. That

was-n't a proph-e-sy, I could just see you were sweat-ing. And I

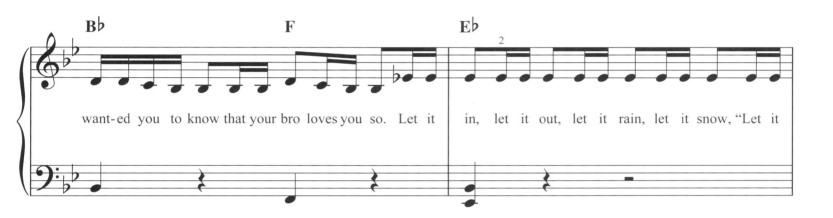

want-ed you to know that your bro loves you so. Let it in, let it out, let it rain, let it snow, "Let it

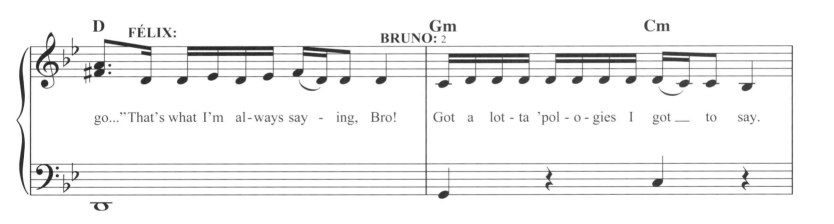

FÉLIX: go..."That's what I'm al-ways say - ing, Bro! BRUNO: Got a lot-ta 'pol-o-gies I got __ to say.

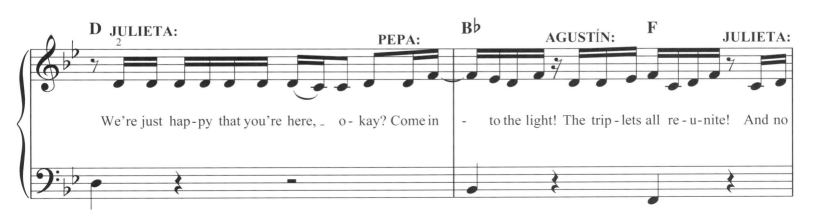

JULIETA: We're just hap-py that you're here, __ o- kay? PEPA: Come in - to the light! AGUSTÍN: The trip-lets all re-u-nite! JULIETA: And no

mat-ter what hap-pens, we're gon-na find _ our way. Yo, I | knew he nev-er left, I heard him ev - 'ry day...

TOWNSPEOPLE:
Oh, _____ oh, _____ | oh, _____ oh. _____

ABUELA ALMA: What's that sound?

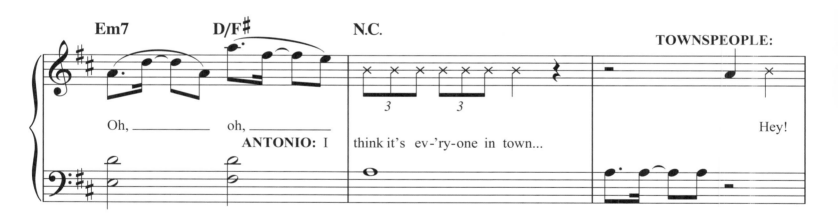

Oh, _____ oh, _____ | ANTONIO: I think it's ev-'ry-one in town... | TOWNSPEOPLE: Hey!

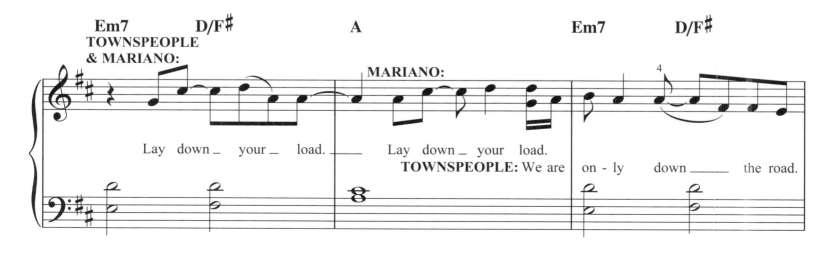

TOWNSPEOPLE & MARIANO:
Lay down _ your _ load. __ | MARIANO: Lay down _ your _ load. | TOWNSPEOPLE: We are on - ly down _____ the road.

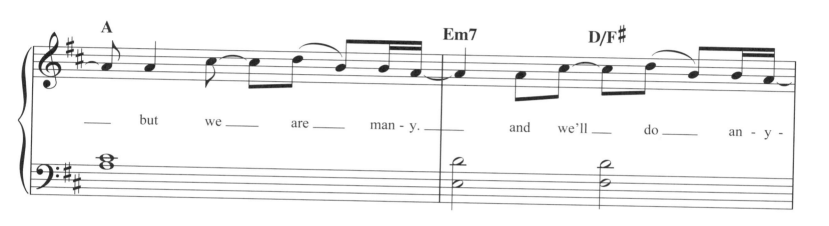

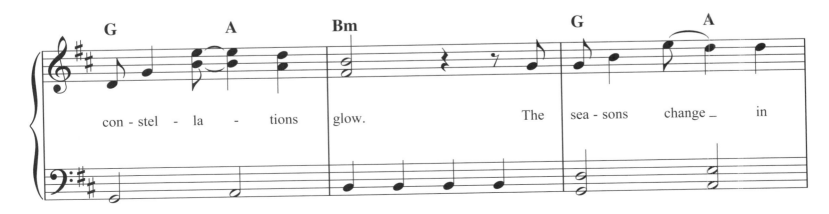

turn. _____ Would you watch our lit-tle girl go? ___ She takes _ af-ter you.

(Mariano sighs) Hey, Mar-i - a - no, why so ___ blue? ___

I just have so much love in - side... Y' know, I've got this cous-in

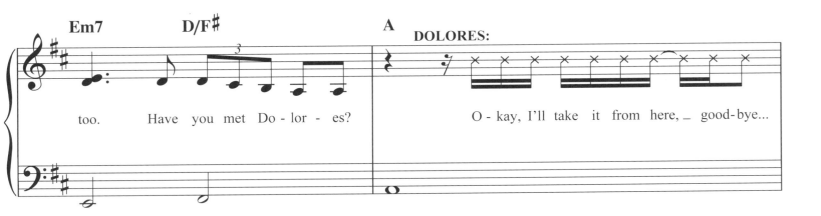

too. Have you met Do - lor - es? O - kay, I'll take it from here, _ good-bye...

You talk so loud. You take care of your moth-er and you make her proud. You

write your own po-et-ry ev-'ry night when you go to sleep. And I'm

seiz-ing the mo-ment, so would you wake up and no-tice me?___

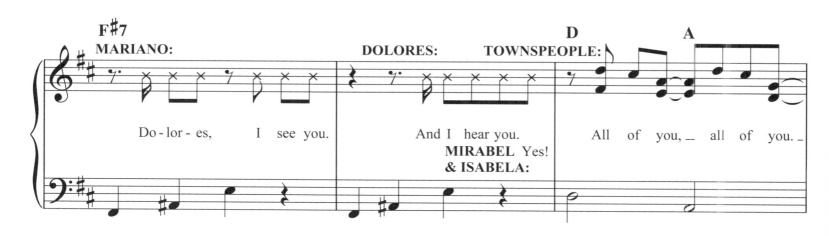

MARIANO: Do-lor-es, I see you.

DOLORES: And I hear you.

TOWNSPEOPLE: All of you,___ all of you.___

MIRABEL & ISABELA: Yes!

66

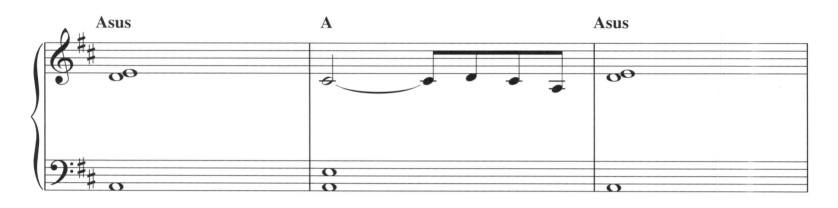

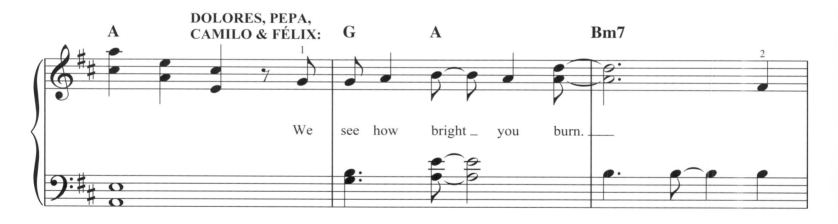

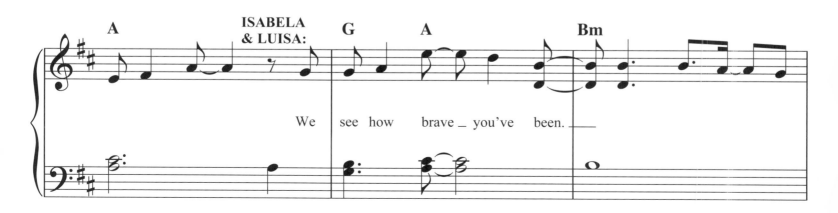

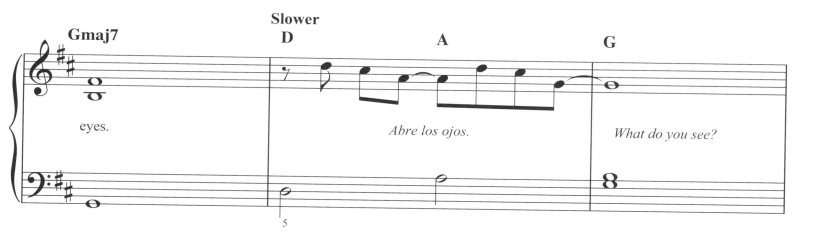

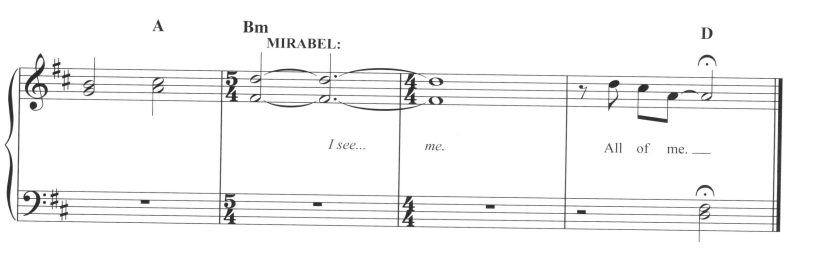

COLOMBIA, MI ENCANTO

Music and Lyrics by
LIN-MANUEL MIRANDA

To Coda ⊕

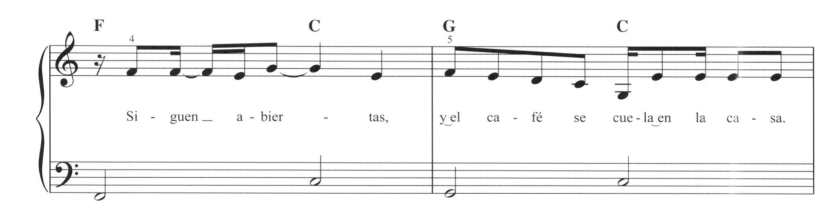

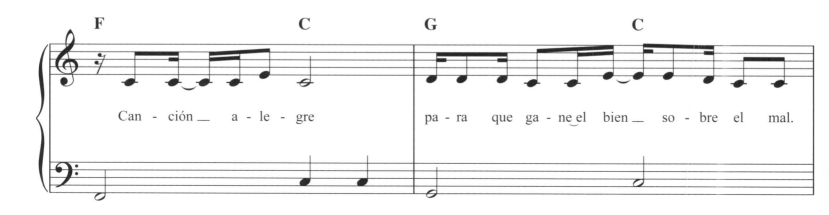

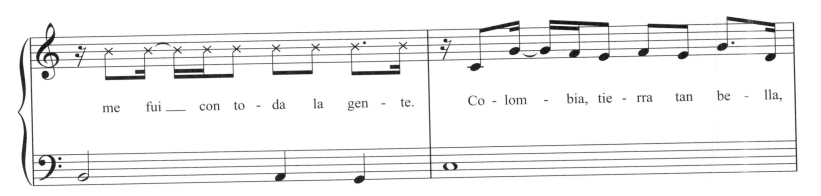

me fui __ con to - da la gen - te. Co - lom - bia, tie - rra tan be - lla,

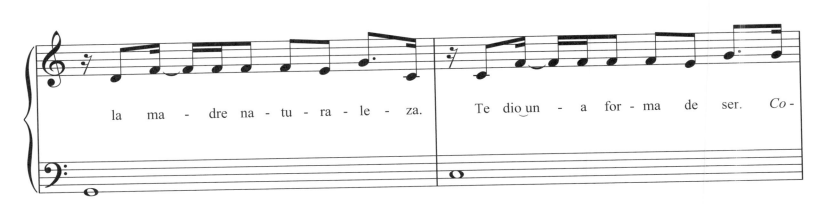

la ma - dre na - tu - ra - le - za. Te dio un - a for - ma de ser. Co-

F   **C**

lom - bi - a stays__ my fa - vor - ite place.__

Co - lom - bia, te qui - e - ro
Y es que a ti Co - lom - bia yo te qui - er - o

G   **F**   **C**

tan - to. _____
tan - to. _____

Que siem - pre me en - a - mo - ra tu en-

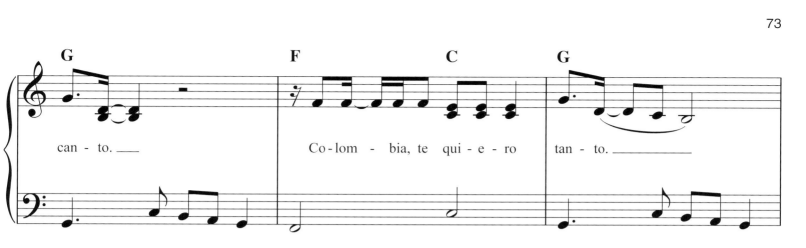

can - to. ___ Co - lom - bia, te qui - e - ro tan - to. _____

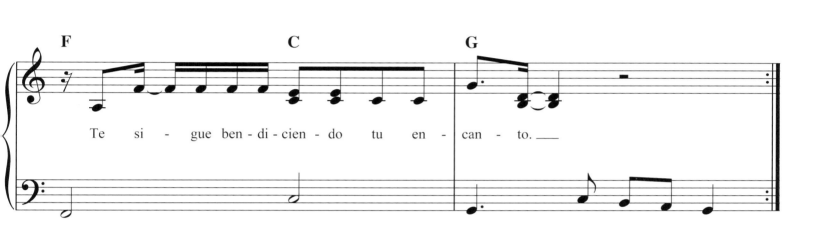

Te si - gue ben - di - cien - do tu en - can - to. ___

En - can - to. En - can -

1. - to.

2. - to.

TWO ORUGUITAS

Music and Lyrics by
LIN-MANUEL MIRANDA

Syncopated groove

Two or - u - gui - tas
Two or - u - gui - tas

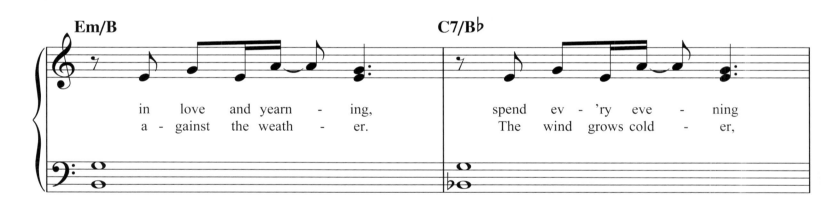

in love and yearn - ing,
a - gainst the weath - er.

spend ev - 'ry eve - ning
The wind grows cold - er,

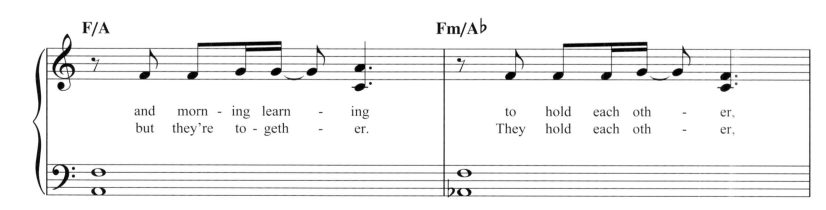

and morn - ing learn - ing
but they're to - geth - er.

to hold each oth - er,
They hold each oth - er,

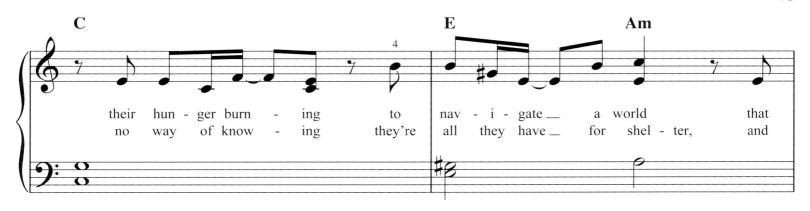

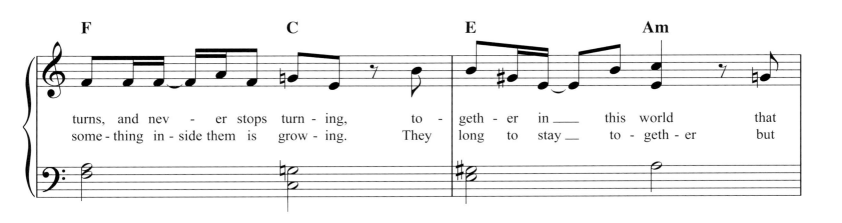

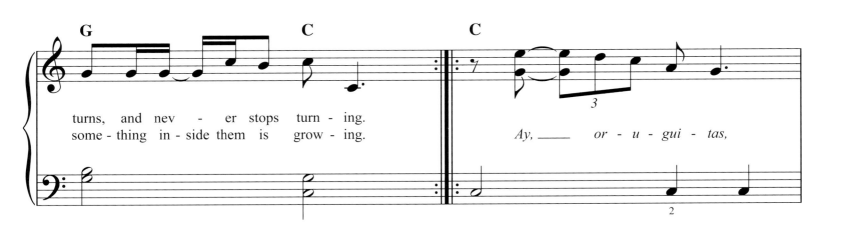

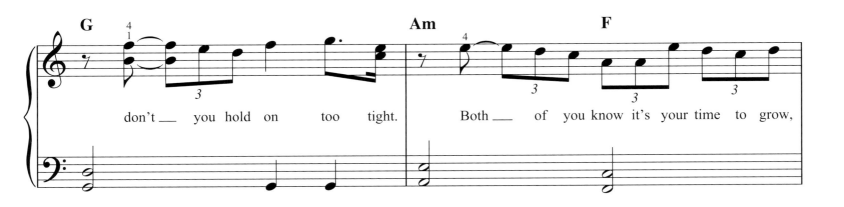

to fall a-part, to re - u - nite. Won - ders a-wait you

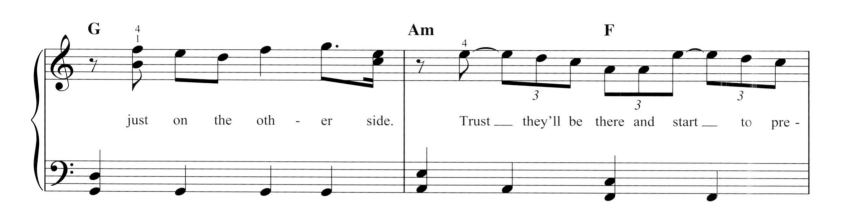

just on the oth - er side. Trust __ they'll be there and start __ to pre -

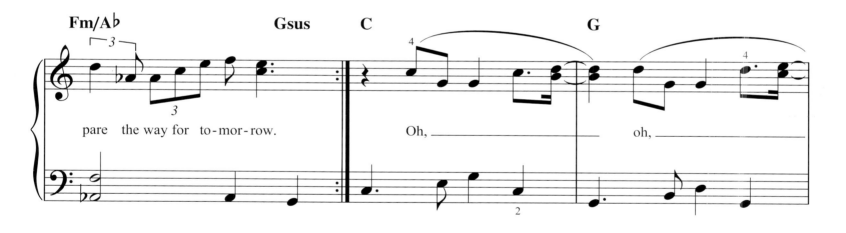

pare the way for to-mor-row. Oh, ___ oh, ___

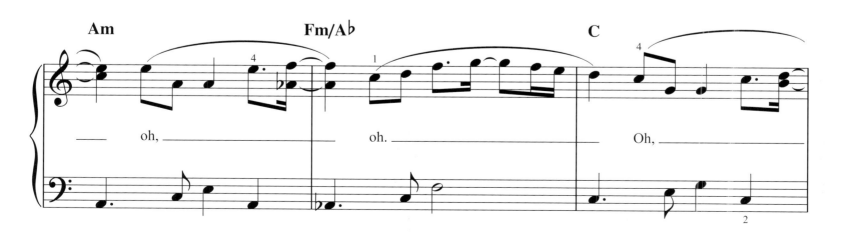

___ oh, ___ oh. Oh, ___

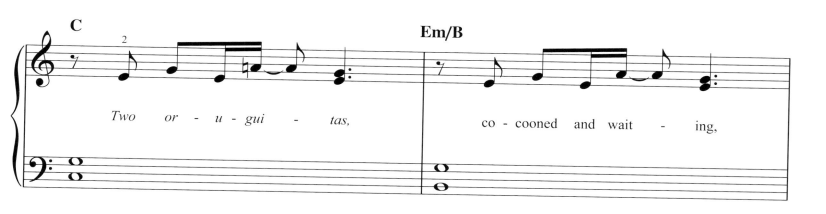

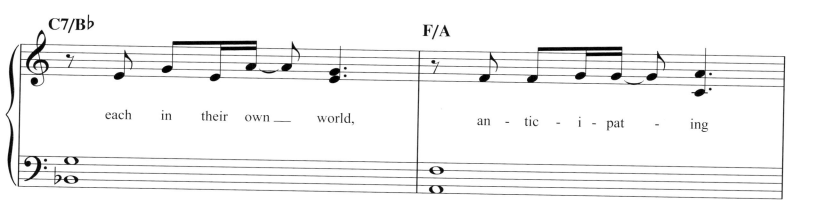

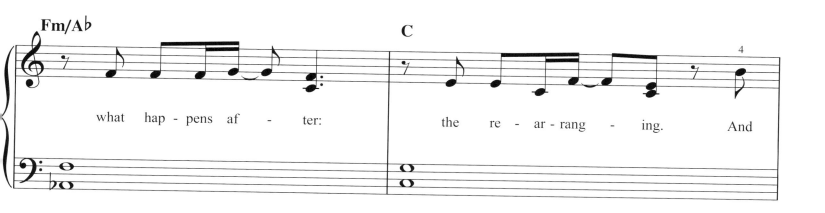

so a-fraid__ of change in a world that nev - er stops chang - ing. So

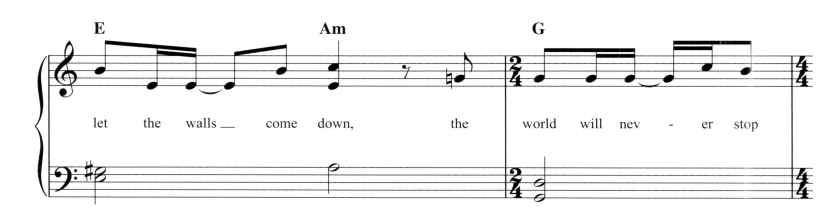

let the walls__ come down, the world will nev - er stop

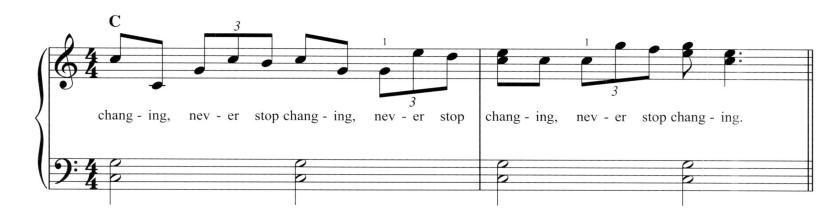

chang - ing, nev - er stop chang - ing, nev - er stop chang - ing, nev - er stop chang - ing.

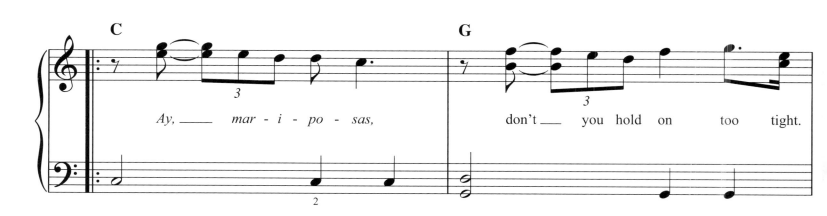

Ay,__ mar - i - po - sas, don't__ you hold on too tight.

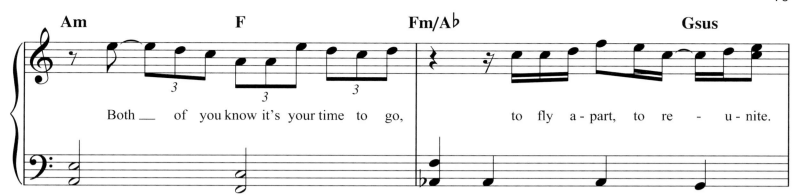

Both __ of you know it's your time to go, to fly a - part, to re - u - nite.

Won - ders sur - round you, just let the walls come down.

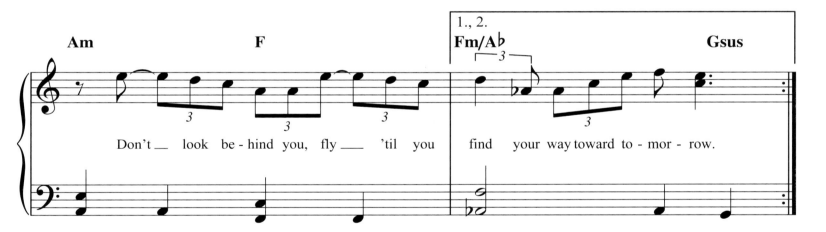

Don't __ look be - hind you, fly __ 'til you find your way toward to - mor - row.

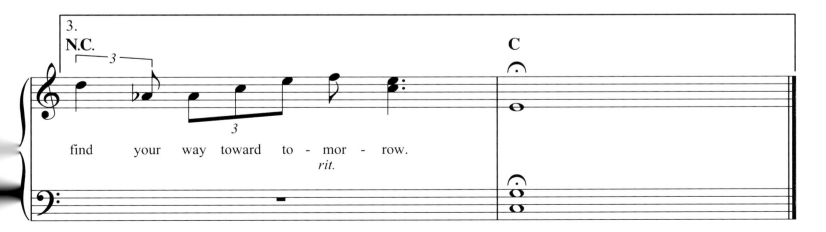

find your way toward to - mor - row.